A Turtle Plants a Village

Written by **Kristin Thiel** & **Peter Tonn** ● Illustrated by **Hannah Tews**

MEQUON *Nature* PRESERVE

Flying three missions in the course of a day
Was nothing new for the Bluejay Jay.
But the cargo shifted, the grip was lost,
Tumbling downward as if perfectly tossed.
Right in the path of a turtle named Bay
Who said, **"What is this that has fallen my way?"**

ROLY POLY

Jay swooped down to recover the seed
And apologized for his clumsy deed,
**"I will bury this acorn deep in the ground.
In several years, something grand will be found."**
Bay looked puzzled and hadn't a clue.
"That sounds like magic. What will it do?"

EARTHWORM

MYCORRHIZAL FUNGI

OAK SEEDLING

Jay explained, "First the roots grow far and wide,
Until a small seedling sprouts up topside.
A seedling's a snack for some passing near
Like a vole, a mouse, and even a deer."
Snacks delighted such a slow crawler,
But Bay wondered more,
"Will it grow taller?"

FIELD MOUSE

WHITE-TAILED DEER

PRAIRIE VOLE

LUNA MOTH

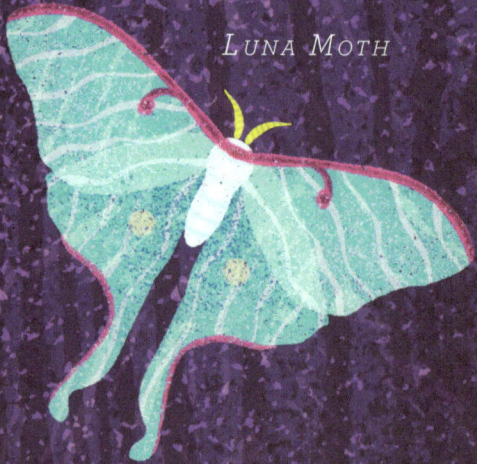

WHITE-TAILED FAWN

Jay replied, "Soon the oak will grow in a hurry.
A new home for bugs and birds
and lots of things furry."
Bay visited the tree many times every year.
It now produced shade for a sleepy young deer.
"This oak is still growing. That's obviously true.
How much can one acorn actually do?"

CARPENTER BEE

OAK SPIDER

The oak reached 20 with a solid trunk base,
Putting a big smile on turtle Bay's face.
"Its leaves are so full, even making a rustle
When winds start to blow showing their muscle.
This village just gets bigger and bigger.
How many new friends will this growth trigger?"

SPRING PEEPER

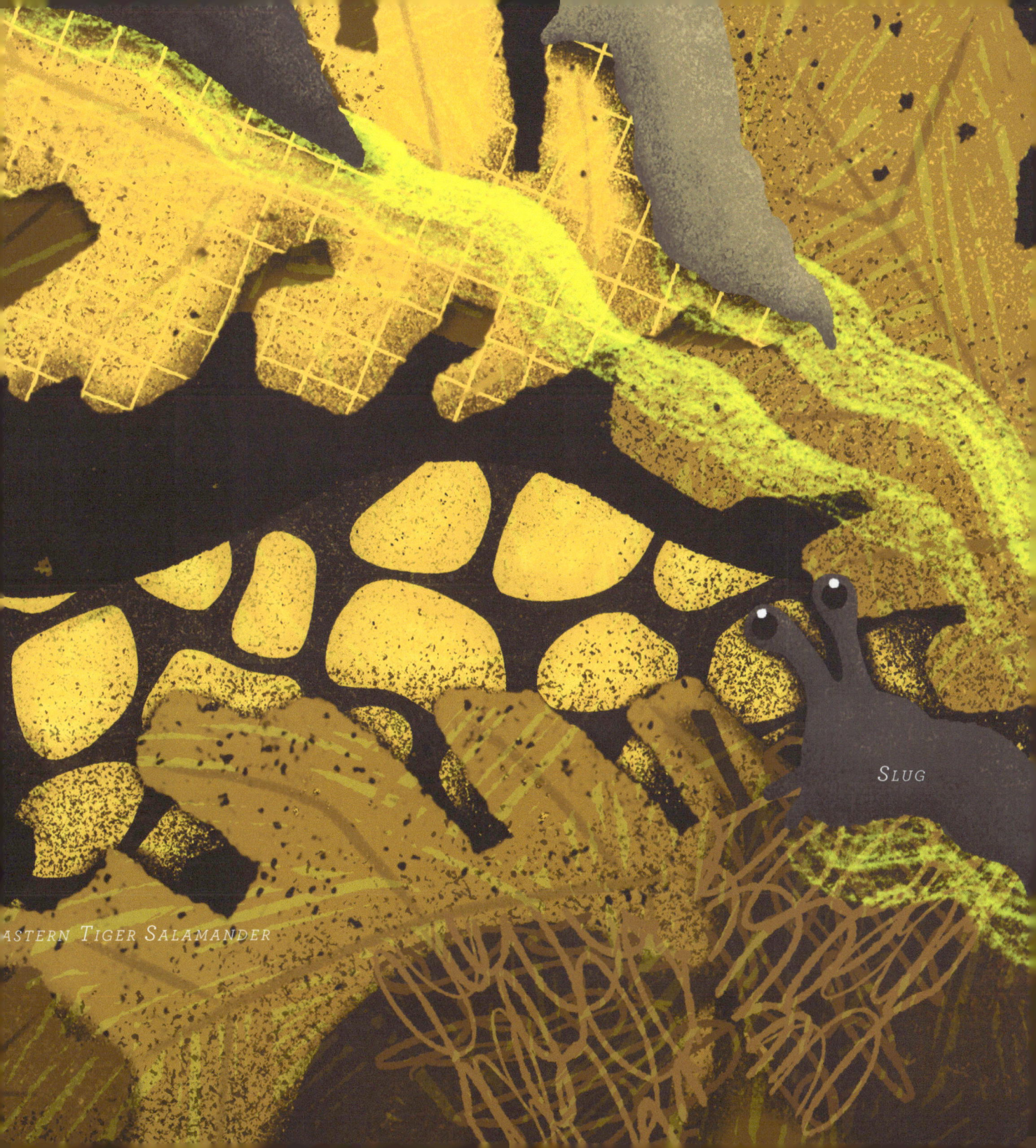

Eastern Tiger Salamander

Slug

The wind picked up with the crack of thunder
As a big branch fell with a thud down under.
A startled Bay had his eyes open wide,
"This broken branch has a home inside!"
The turtle looked over the branch that had broke
Wondering, **"Who else lives up high in this oak?"**

EASTERN GRAY SQUIRREL

"I do, for one," said a squirrel named Gray.
"I've got to make sure my drey is okay.
Want a ride up to the top of the tree?
Just hop onto my tail and climb with me.
Meet some of my friends living up in the sky."
"I will," said Bay. "There's a new world up high?"

Bay's first stop: a cavity in the trunk
Made the perfect spot for four owls to bunk.
"Whoo are you?" asked the Great Horned mother.
"You're quite different from most of the others."
"My name is Bay Turtle and I live aground.
Do you have friendly neighbors hanging around?"

GREAT HORNED OWL

GREAT HORNED OWLET

CICADA EXOSKELETON

Bay was directed a few branches down
Where a nuthatch, a bug, and a brown bat were found.
Exploring still further, Bay discovered much more,
Such as moths, gull wasps and small predators.
"What a colorful world and a busy one, too!"
Declared turtle Bay with excitement. "Who knew?"

NUTHATCH

SPONGY MOTH CATERPILLAR

ANTS

OAK GALL

BROWN BAT

Bay now admired Jay's work with applause.
This home for so many was a genuine cause.
An opossum strolled by with a frown on its face,
Asking Bay, "Aren't you a bit out of place?"
"The wetlands are where I'm usually found.
Can I grab onto your tail if you're going down?"

Back on the ground, Bay's head was spinning,
With a huge happy smile, more than just grinning.
**"An oak has the power to provide for so many.
I need an acorn to start, yet I haven't any."**
A flutter of wings was then heard overhead.
"Whoo will get a new home?" the Great Owl said.

Bay balanced the acorn high on his shell
And waved goodbye with a fond farewell.
Grabbing a shovel and a backpack, too,
Bay headed for prairie and into the blue.
After hiking awhile came a moment of zen,
"Now it's time to plant.
If not now, when?"

BUSTLING BURR OAKS

Fun Facts

Oak Trees • are the best trees to plant in your yard to support wildlife. There are 950 different kinds of caterpillars that need oak trees to survive. With 91 different types of oak trees across the country, there is definitely at least one that would be perfect for your yard!

Roly Polys (or Pill Bugs) • are critical in helping the environment as they are one of the number one bugs that help decompose materials. Think of them as nature's recyclers!

Oak Seedling • This powerful young oak is an important food source for many different animals like deer, mice, squirrels and birds!

Earthworm • Also a nature recycler, helps break down debris in the soil all while creating spaces for water to enter the soil and reach the roots of plants. Earthworms can live up to 20 years old!

Mycorrhizal fungi • are powerhouses that help plants grow, improve soil health and help keep plants living a stress-free life.

Field Mouse • is a tiny mammal found all over North America and Europe and loves to live under or in the fallen branches in the forest.

White-tailed Deer • can normally be seen munching on food like oak seedlings at dawn or twilight. Sometimes it's hard for us to see them, but they can see you! Deer have excellent eyesight and hearing.

Fawn • is the name for a young white-tailed deer. Fawns always have white spots on their backs to help them hide in nature. These spots fade after the fawn is about 6-12 months old.

Prairie Voles • are little mammals that are very social and love to spend time with their families. Male and female voles stay paired for life.

Carpenter Bees • are very large bees that look li a Bumble bee, but they are not. They live in tunnels th they create in wood. These bees are truly talented at making perfect circles in the wood that look exactly like something a drill made.

Luna Moth • is a beautiful, large moth nicknamed Moon Moth. If you see this moth in your yard or loca natural area, it is a sign of a healthy ecosystem as thes insects are sensitive and cannot live everywhere.

Oak Spider • is only found in Europe, but the beaut pattern on its back looks like the shape of an oak lea

Spring Peepers • are tiny frogs the size of a finger and have the earliest frog calls you will hear in the fore of the Midwest. The high-pitched "peeps" are comin from the male frogs trying to attract a female friend

Slug • is another insect that i an important nature recycler. A slug is also a great pollinator often collecting pollen from one flower on its sticky bo and dropping the pollen on another flower.

Eastern Tiger Salamander • is one of the larg salamanders in North America. These critters will retu to where they were born to have their babies.

Walking Sticks • are best known for, well ... looking like a stick! The extremely unique body make them highy effective in hiding in the trees of a forest One of nature's best camouflage!

Eastern Gray Squirrels • are mammals that are super active during the day, usually found eating. Because of its large appetite, it is an important critte that helps regenerate or regrow forests!

Oak Leaf Caterpillars • are tiny caterpillars th feed on the leaves and flowers of oak trees.

Great Horned Owlets • are fuzzy babies that will grow up to be incredible hunters. They are born blind, making them helpless and needing to stay close to the nest and their parents.

Great Horned Owls • are strong and fast hunters with excellent night vision. The "horns" on its head are just tufts of feathers that look like horns to help camouflage the bird and scare away predators.

Cicada Exoskeleton • is the hard outer covering that once was on the body of a cicada. Cicada's shed this over as they grow and turn into the adult form with wings.

Oak Gall • Don't be alarmed by these beautifully weird growths on the leaves of the oak trees. They come in many shapes, sizes and colors, and are all caused by the tree's reaction to a gall wasp laying its eggs in the tree leaves.

Brown Bats • are mammals only active at night and live in the canopy of the trees. If you see one flying around, you're lucky as they are usually sleeping about 20 hours a day!

Ants • are tiny, but mighty. Ants can life up to 50 times their body weight. That's like a man carrying an adult cow!

Spongy Moth Caterpillar • is an insect that isn't very good for the native trees of North America, as its home is Asia. With too many of these caterpillars, the tree leaves could all be eaten!

Nuthatches • are entertaining birds that love to feed on spiders and insects, so they love oak trees for the variety of food. They are entertaining since they hop headfirst up and down the trunks of trees, making them fun to watch!

Published by Orange Hat Publishing 2025
HC ISBN: 9781645386469

Copyright © 2025 by Kristin Thiel and Peter Tonn
All Rights Reserved
A Turtle Plants a Village
Written by Kristin Thiel and Peter Tonn
Illustrated by Hannah Tews

OrangeHat
PUBLISHING
orangehatpublishing.com

Mequon Nature Preserve is
a 510-acre active land restoration
site and living laboratory where you can
explore, discover, breathe, learn and help restore
5 different ecosystems. There are no trail fees, no
membership fees, just come enjoy, reconnect with the
land and watch the transformation happen right before
your eyes. Just 20 years into a 150-year restoration plan,
80,000 trees and shrubs have been planted. Thirty acres of
wetland restored and hundreds of native wildlife and plant
species are now thriving thanks to donors,
community partners, and volunteers who all
come together in concert to make this
incredible transformation possible.

www.ingramcontent.com/pod-product-compliance
Lightning Source LLC
Chambersburg PA
CBHW040740150426
42813CB00064B/2966

* 9 7 8 1 6 4 5 3 8 6 4 6 9 *